SANYAOLU
KEHINDE & TAIWO

HOLE IN THE POCKET
MILLIONAIRES

SIX PERSONAL FINANCE MISTAKES FROM CELEBRITIES GONE BANKRUPT AND HOW YOU CAN AVOID THEM

Stakes Capital
Lagos, Nigeria

Published by Stakes Capital Ltd
4, Olufeko close, Fola Agoro, Shomolu, Lagos Nigeria.
Website: www.stakescapital.com.
Email: letstalk@stakescapital.com   Tel: +2348054061133

Research contributions courtesy International Corporate Research Nigeria, a Stakes Capital Ltd brand. www.icr.stakescapital.com
www.hipmillionaires.com

A catalogue record of this book is available from the National Library of Nigeria.

1st print: February 2014

ISBN: 9789789333691

Printed in the United States of America

dedication

To those who by reason of use have had their senses
trained to descern between good and evil

acknowledgement

Some persons, having been well tutored by life, have enough deft to smell a worthy course a mile away. Thanks to all those who criticized, made commendations and made financial commitments

foreword

Money is like a spirit. Without discipline or a clear strategy for dealing with it the money can take control and deal with us. Kehinde and Taiwo Sanyaolu reflected on those who had it all and lost it and offer counsel on how to avoid such a fate.

Why is their counsel worthwhile? The twins are consummate researchers who have followed the rich and powerful on issues including money disorders and knowledge for living. The examples; from pitfalls into which many celebrities descend and squander their wealth form the basis for financial planning tips we could all use to ensure discipline when we experience a sudden outbreak of riches.

Taiwo and Kehinde offer us a handy companion handbook in an easy reading form such that we have fun learning how not to make the mistakes others have made. The six pitfalls they identify and the guide to investments for the novice help make people "boy scouts" of personal wealth management. As with scouting, the charge is "Be prepared."

Patrick Okedinachi Utomi
Professor of Political Economy and Entrepreneurship was Director of the Center for applied Economics at the Lagos Business School and is founder of the Center for Applied Economics

testimonies

Multiple source of income may sound like an economic jargon to the uninitiated. To those who know, it's not just a financial golden key it is the reason they remain the successful celebrity that remains on top of their game. This book is not just a book it is a bible for every young man and woman who wants to block financial leakages and get out of pits that bury the great talents that abound in every sector in our country. If I may add, this book is a saving grace. **Ali Baba, Africa's King of comedy**

This is a child of necessity and very timely because the entertainment industry is picking up fast. The industry is different now; talent truly expires. The lifespan of the average entertainer is very short now than before so it is important to learn from the examples of others. This book has helped me personally to understand the business of my hobby. The book is absolutely needed. **DJ Jimmy Jatt, Renowned Disc Jockey**

Growing up, we are encouraged to read up and equip ourselves with financial knowledge. However, most documents, journals and even books speak above our heads, they speak to the financially inclined. This book bridges a gap between the two, it speaks to all. By providing vital financial principles and real life experiences, this book is an interesting over view of how finances can go right or very wrong. Every young person hoping to make a financial mark should read this book. **Rorisang Thandekiso, Head of Content Planet RadioTV South Africa (Good Morning Africa)**

A celebrity's brand value and continued public relevance is tied closely to his consistent financial success. This book strongly enforces this truth with its case studies. Many industry colleges and other celebrities would have had better financial success if they had read this book at a point in their career. **Saint Obi, Ace Actor**

To be moneywise can never be overemphasized. This book is a factual record of examples to help anyone learn the 'how to's' of drawing from their pocket without making holes. It will make an interesting read for many. **Tosin Martins, Ace Musician**

The 6 pitfalls highlighted in the book "Hole in the pocket Millionaires" encapsulates every professional entertainers nightmares. The book is a must read for any Celebrity who plans not to make the journey from 'Superstardom to Super-liability'. Great job. **Okey 'Bakassi', Renowned Comic**

There is nothing as important as learning. History itself is a tapestry of learning. There is a saying that 'there is nothing new under the sun', so as long as you are willing to learn you don't need to make the same mistakes other people have made. Create a new history! **Omotunde Davies - Lolo 1 of Wazobia fm, On Air Personality**

This is one of the most insightful books I have ever read, it comes with exact facts and figures to drive home its points and I have learnt a whole lot from reading it, the perfect financial adviser to every celebrity making money. The book is a must have. **Owen Gee, Ace Comedian**

Anybody can stumble into 'success' but not everyone can 'stay in success'. It takes self-disciple and hard work to 'stay in success'. Sometimes the price we have to pay to remain successful is more compared to just breaking into it. This is a must read for all 'celebs' out there. This is one topic nobody is talking about yet there is a clear evidence of holes in pockets! It's a great job by the authors. **Sam Adekunbi, Resident minister, KICC Lekki, Lagos**

The writing is simple and makes it easy to comprehend. The nuggets are also very true. I have observed a few things I should change in my life already. **Roxanne Rouse, Fashion entrepreneur**

This is a perspective changer and an eye opener for celebrities. It is simple, educative and easy to understand. The notion that business books are a bore is defused when you read hole in the pocket millionaires. **Saco comedian**

If you want to make it as an entertainer you need two things – talent and this book. **Dom Lawson, Artist manager**

This book will give celebrities all the knowledge they need about financial planning so that we celebrities can stop living the false life that drives many into bankruptcy. **Michael Lawrence (Ogbolo), Comic and OAP**

content

LIST OF CELEBRITY SPOTLIGHTS

∽ · ∾

SHOW TIME

*T*here is hardly anyone who comes into the world with a definite desire to be poor. You never have to ask why wealth is simply a better deal naturally. So has the world of man been designed - in favor of those who possess wealth.

The most delectable[1] to human taste and all that will arrest his fancy are the priciest in commerce. The princely robes he desires to be clothed with, the mesmeric[2] automobiles he would love to be chauffeured in, the noble abode he would love to call home and even the pristine[3] beaches where he would rather seek to be recreated will demand the most from his purse.

―――――――――――― DICTIONARY

1 Delectable: Extremely pleasing to taste
2 Mesmeric: Attracting and holding interest as if by a spell
3 Pristine: Immaculate, clean, pure, dirt free

This desire for wealth and the best it can buy is bequeathed naturally to all. To the off-spring of the rich it comes in no greater measure than to those sired[4] by a beggar.

Rarely does any activity proceed without the need to employ money at some point. Money is the store of value, the principal means of exchange and the tool that helps to achieve all things with only whit[5] exceptions. Perhaps, *'money answers all things'* is a succinct[6] conclusion.

Little wonder most predefined life activities are designed to pitch an individual against a penurious[7] end.

According to John Gills, author of the monumental exposition of the bible,

'Money is in the room of all things, and by it men obtain everything they want and wish for; it answers the requests of all, and supplies them with what they stand in need of, or can desire: it is the sinew[8] of war when it arises, and will procure men and arms, to secure and protect him from his enemies, and obtain peace and safety for him and his subjects'.

DICTIONARY

4 Sire: Father; make children
5 Whit: A tiny or scarcely detectable amount
6 Succinct: Summary; briefly giving the gist of something
7 Penurious: Not having enough money to pay for necessities
8 Sinew: Quality of having muscular strength

In pursuit of wealth

Anyone who regards poverty a worthy companion is at best considered palsied[9] in his mind. So daily across the world it's a crazy jostle[10] in pursuit of wealth, more of it every day we all seek. For the poor, he is driven by the cold and hunger of the previous night and the rich, a never ending appetite for more.

Tonnes of books have been written to aid this quest for wealth, a journey for some and perpetuation[11] for others. One of such is *Empire of Business* a 1907 classic by Andrew Carnegie - American industrialist and philanthropist and founder of the iron and steel industry in the United States, who is noted for his many charitable gifts. In it he posited[12] that *'wealth is the business of the world'*.

This assertion arose from the fact that, *'except for few exceptions, men are born to poverty and therefore always seek what to do for the community to earn him enough wealth to feed, clothe, shelter and keep him independent of charitable aid from others'*. Invariably, money is at the base of continuing human existence, interaction and purposefulness.

No matter how rich you may have grown, there's always a greater cause for which money can be applied.

—————————— DICTIONARY

9 Palsy: Paralysis; Loss of the ability to move a body part
10 Jostle: Force your way by pushing
11 Perpetuation: The act of prolonging something
12 Posited: Take as a given; assume as a postulate or axiom

Everyone, regardless of the quantity he currently possesses must therefore amass some more money because money is the means by which we may fulfill our purpose in a larger and better way and achieve more sophisticated taste.

Therefore, who needs an education on why wealth should be sought, man's natural appetite pulls him into the insuppressible hustle[13] for economic power.

Cumulatively, the greatest volume of time and energy expended is in one form of economic activity or another. In today's economy and certainly those of ages gone by, nothing is more feared than the threat of poverty and nothing seems more arduous[14] than the task of earning a new penny.

A little work, a lot more money... so it seems

The natural course is that much wealth is begat by commensurate[15] labor; same appears to be the reality. Even to earn a little, you have to put in a lot; to earn more, a lot more is demanded of you.

In some industries however, individuals appear to be earning more by exploiting their natural talent, a resource they did not labor for. Though they put in a lot as well, their outrageous[16]

—————————————— DICTIONARY

13 Hustle: Get by trying hard
14 Arduous: Difficult to accomplish; demanding considerable mental effort and skill
15 Commensurate: Corresponding in size, degree or extent
15 Outrageous: Greatly exceeding bounds of reason or moderation

earnings appear to dwarf whatever effort they may have put into their work. They earn so much, a life-time could be secured financially in a pretty short time. Some of such are entertainers and sports stars – celebrities as they are more commonly referred.

Man's unrestrained appetite for entertainment has made these industries money spinners any day any time. Any activity that possesses even an iota of entertainment is always more enchanting[17] and fascinating.

The movies, sports, comedy, music etc. command huge attention. Many rich corporations seeking to promote their services/products and extend their brands also show a lot of interest, stepping in with lots of cash accompanying.

In 2007, PricewaterhouseCoopers - *Pwc* in its *'global entertainment & media market outlook report'* said the industry will hit $2 trillion by 2011.

According to annual surveys concerning the size of the sports business industry, it is estimated to reach a value of $213 billion. *Pwc* though suggesting a more conservative[18] figure said that the sports industry was worth $114 billion in 2010 projected to hit 133billion by 2013.

—————————— DICTIONARY

17 Enchanting: Capturing interest as if by a spell
18 Conservative: Avoiding excess

Doesn't appear to be all rosy...

The major players who have made a career out of these (sports and entertainment) are the better for it as they share of the endless flow of wealth available in form of exorbitant salaries and corporate endorsements.

However, good earnings do not always translate to financial security. In 2008, the NBA Players Association claimed that 60% of professional basketball players go broke within 5 years of retirement some going bankrupt[19] even before their careers approach its end. *Sports Illustrated* also said almost 80% of National Football League players are flirting with bankruptcy two years after they retire.

It is therefore not out of place to discuss guarding your wealth from loss and how you can perpetuate your wealth to prevent a slip back to penury[20]. For a man who earns only enough to feed himself with a meal undeserving of men of taste, he would eat his meal in thanks because he knows no better taste.

But what could be more enervating[21] than slipping into lack from abundance; for a man who has eaten off the table of nobility to seek to share of the plate of have-nots.

———————————— DICTIONARY

19 Bankrupt: Financially ruined
20 Penury: A state of extreme poverty or destitution
21 Enervating: Causing debilitation - serious weakening and loss of energy

Late in 2010, *cnbc.com* producer Daniel Bukszpan posted a feature on '15 musicians gone broke', highlighting how men and women who had risen to mega-stardom and earning megabucks now live broke. As though to shed more light on the precarious[22] situation, he again in April 2011 featured a list of '15 top athletes who had gone bankrupt'.

Yeah! Shit happens, but the last place you should let it happen is in your finances. Imagine the horror of not being able to feed as you used to, clothe the way you desire or live your luxurious life anymore. Think about the shame that will accompany the tabloid headlines deriding[23] your financial crash, your family, friends, colleagues etc. and how you would be unable to face the public again.

A number of things are common to them all; the obvious ones being that they all made it to the peak of their careers, earned big and eventually went bankrupt. However, between their huge salaries and the final crash into debt are also rarely talked about financial blunders, obvious from careful study, which made their end predictable.

So what do we do about this?

The focus of this book is to expose these pitfalls and draw critical lessons that if adhered to will help you forestall finding

---

DICTIONARY

22 Precarious: Affording no ease or reassurance
23 Deride: Treat or speak of with contempt; mock

yourself in their shoes sooner or later in your life.

That you are earning a lot now is really of no consequence because most of these guys earned record breaking salaries in their active years. Earning large has proven time and again to be an ineffective shield against financial distress, instead the financial management skills that this book teaches are dependable armor for the discerning.

The lessons have been drawn with celebrities and other high earners in mind and offers simple usable tips that will help uphold your hard earned wealth. It is extremely important that you take these lessons to heart and put to practice as you seek to build a fortified[24] financial future.

It is a tragedy of monumental proportion for a man to have earned so much and yet be unable to hold on to his wealth.

The following are the financial mistakes we have discovered to resonate through every celebrity who has gone from grace to grass and others en route bankruptcy.

_____ DICTIONARY

24 Fortified: Secured

PITFALL 1

THEY SPEND
FRIVOLOUSLY

CELEBRITY SPOTLIGHT

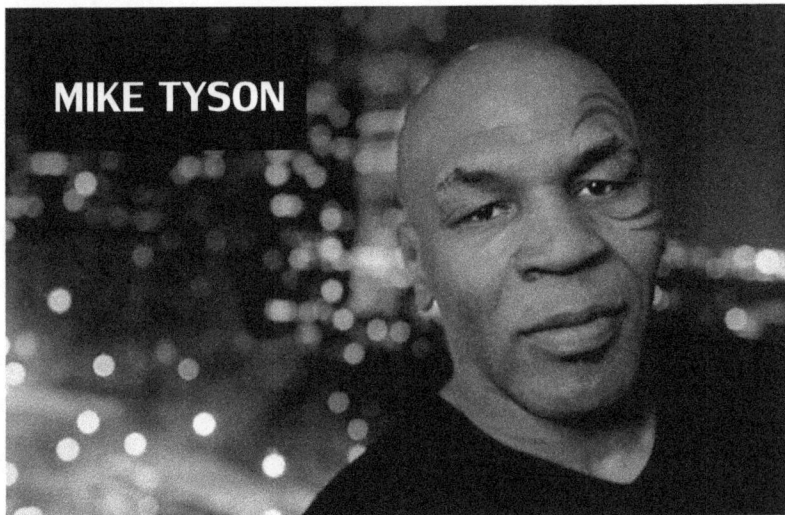

MIKE TYSON

Mike Tyson is a former undisputed heavyweight champion of the world and holds the record as the youngest boxer to win the WBC, WBA and IBF world heavyweight titles, he was 20 years, 4 months and 22 days old. For a while, no boxer on earth was as feared as "Iron Mike" Tyson. Tyson won his first 19 professional bouts by knockout, with twelve of them occurring in the first round. He won the WBC title in 1986 after defeating Trevor Berbick by a TKO in the second round. In 1987, Tyson added the WBA and IBF titles after defeating James Smith and Tony Tucker. He was the first heavyweight boxer to simultaneously hold and only Heavyweight to individually unify the WBA, WBC and IBF titles.

Money shouldn't have been a problem for Tyson. After all, according to the *New York Times*, he had earned more than $400 million in his boxing career. However, he had spent almost all of it, frittering it away on extravagances like mansions, luxury cars and pet tigers. He also owed $9 million for his divorce settlement and $13 million to the IRS. When he filed for bankruptcy in 2003, he claimed debts of $27 million.

$\mathcal{F}$or almost every movie star, sports star, A-list comedian or music star, success is usually sudden. Not so much the rise to stardom (many usually achieve it through careful diligence and years of hard painstaking commitment to their careers), but the escalation[25] in their earning to unimagined levels.

Many of them been unprepared for such quickly take to luxurious living. Perhaps spurred[26] by an emotional spite for their previous states of lack, they are so blinded by where they are coming from that they cannot see where they are headed. *Los Angeles Dodgers* manager Tommy Lasorda once marveled about his talented pitcher Fernando Valenzuela, *"many star athletes from impoverished backgrounds have great difficulty adjusting to fucking star salaries"*.

With financial planning, prudence or foresightedness virtually nonexistent to many, consuming becomes the order and very soon they are given away to frittering[27] by their insatiable appetite.

The reason for this is usually traced to the fact that celebrities live a public life and are usually in public glare courtesy of the media. The media, being what they are, soar their public

---

DICTIONARY

25 Escalation: An increase (in seriousness, price, cost, etc.)
26 Spur: Incite or stimulate
27 Fritter: Spend frivolously and unwisely

image and portray them as figures that are larger than life[28], which rarely has an ultimate advantage.

Living to this façade[29] therefore, becomes the preoccupation of most celebrities who must daily act in concordance to impress their numerous admirers and must at no time appear tarnished before the paparazzi[30].

They spend frivolously on clothes, jewelry and other bodily adornments. Often some of these raiment and accessories are worn just once before they are condemned to the wardrobe, again in faithful allegiance to public expectations not to repeat cloths.

This frivolous spending habit is also fueled by the inimical[31] and fatally wrong philosophy that money is made to be spent. And spend they do until they spend in excess of what they earn or can possibly earn.

They believe they are supposed to dine in exclusive places, drive exotic automobiles, shop at luxury stores... falling prey to living a life they cannot afford or maintain. Because a tainted[32] public image is a luxury no celebrity would want to

---

28 Larger-than-life: Very imposing or impressive; surpassing the ordinary
29 Façade: A showy misrepresentation intended to conceal something unpleasant
30 Paparazzi: A freelance photographer who pursues celebrities trying to take candid photographs of them to sell to newspapers or magazines
31 Inimical: Not friendly, unfavorable
32 Tainted: Touched by rot or decay; contaminated

stake a dime on, they tag along with the wild expectations of the public by living to impress less impressive people.

Some celebrities are themselves given to wild tastes; they spend their earnings on many things they can do without and would usually pay usurious[33] amounts for less valuable items in the name of class.

They follow trends and vogue without reason while luxury goods manufacturers who exploit this weakness to sell their, many a time, irrelevant products find viable markets among imprudent[34] celebrities.

With such slippery spending habits it wouldn't be long before bankruptcy and its army come at them with guns blazing[35].

DICTIONARY

33 Usurious: Greatly exceeding bounds of reason or moderation
34 Imprudent: Lacking wise self-restraint
35 With guns blazing: In a determined aggressive way

CELEBRITY SPOTLIGHT

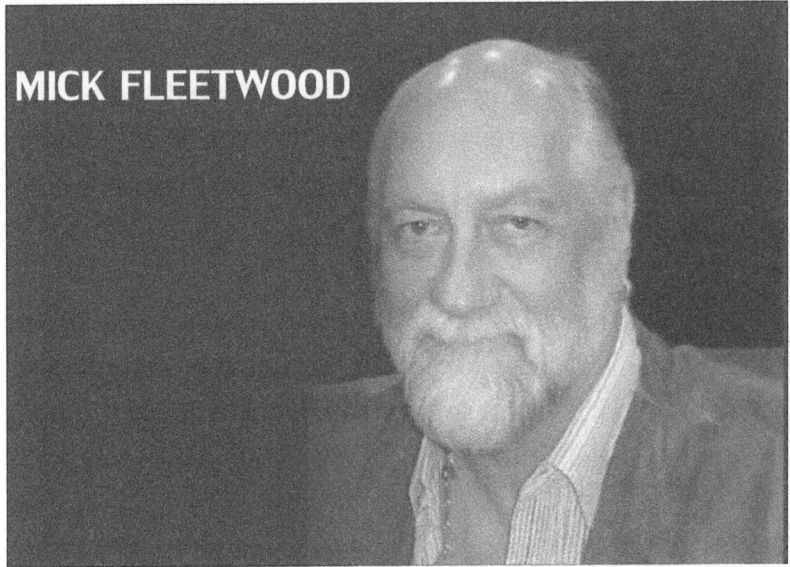

MICK FLEETWOOD

Mick Fleetwood is a British musician and actor best known for his role as the drummer and namesake of the blues/rock and roll band Fleetwood Mac. best known for the hit 1977 album *Rumors*.

As one of the best selling records of all time, the performance royalties alone should have had the drummer set up for life, but he spent his money as quickly as he got it, buying millions of dollars in real estate and using cocaine to the tune of several thousand dollars per month.

By his own estimate, Fleetwood's years of nose candy consumption cost him roughly $8 million, and by 1984 all of his money was gone. With the debts insurmountable, Mick Fleetwood filed for personal bankruptcy, and it would take him almost ten years to get back on his feet again. The drummer has been clean and sober since 1991.

What should you do differently?

*T*he first and basic advice is that financial planning should be a critical part of your life. Financial planning is the process of wisely managing your finances so you can achieve your goals and dreams, while at the same time negotiating the financial barriers that inevitably arise in every stage of life.

To effectively plan your finances you should first understand and accept the fact that you will not always earn from your current primary engagement. The peculiarity of the entertainment industry which is totally given to trends and new talent should guide you to knowing that you will not always be in high demand.

Every celebrity has his peak periods and peak periods don't last forever; new talents are discovered daily, preferences change, injuries occur, scandals happen and also age will definitely set in to knock you off the scene.

At some point your earnings from your career will diminish almost totally. Even Michael Jackson the acclaimed king of pop music, years before his death had ceased in relevance and consequently didn't earn as much from his music career as when he was at his peak.

Realizing that you will not continue to earn as much as you currently do from your career is the mentality that will serve as the foundation you'd need to build a life of financial prudence.

Even though your taste has not changed, neither has the temptation to live the celebrity lifestyle diminished but once your thought is tuned to this realization, you will be better able to manage your mundane[36] desires.

The basic foundation for financial prudence is planning; learn to plan your expenses always. Recall the famous quote by British politician and statesman Winston Churchill during World War II, *"He who fails to plan is planning to fail"*. Harvey Mackay in a revision similar to this said, *"Failures don't plan to fail; they fail to plan"*.

You should understand that financial planning is all about securing your future financial state by maximizing the value you get from your present earnings. Therefore, do not live as though there is no tomorrow, you should get thinking and decide what goals you'd want to achieve financially.

You'd want to be able to continue feeding well, clothing well, living well, pay your bills, support your parents, educate your kids and donate to some charitable work even long after your career years. You therefore need to be tactical financially. (See financial planning tips on page 61)

─────────────── DICTIONARY

36 Mundane: Concerned with the world or worldly matters

PITFALL 2

THEY LIVE BEYOND
THEIR MEANS

CELEBRITY SPOTLIGHT

MICHAEL JACKSON

Michael Joseph Jackson was an American recording artist, dancer, singer-songwriter, musician, and philanthropist. Referred to as the *King of Pop*, Jackson is recognized as the most successful entertainer of all time by Guinness World Records. Jackson's 1982 album *Thriller* is the best-selling album of all time. His other records, including *Off the Wall* (1979), *Bad* (1987), *Dangerous* (1991), and *HIStory* (1995), also rank among the world's best-selling. In 1989, his annual earnings from album sales, endorsements, and concerts were estimated at $125 million for that year alone.

In March 1988, Jackson purchased Neverland Ranch at a cost of $17 million. He installed Ferris wheels, a menagerie, and a movie theater on the 2,700-acre (11 km^2) property. A security staff of 40 patrolled the grounds. In March 2006, the main house at the Neverland Ranch was closed as a *cost-cutting measure*. Jackson had been delinquent on his repayments of a $270 million loan secured against his music publishing holdings, even though those holdings were reportedly making him as much as $75 million a year. There was more than reason to believe that Michael Jackson was on the precipice of bankruptcy. He was described as a *"spendaholic"* who *"has a billionaire spending habit for only a millionaire's spending budget"*.

$\mathcal{M}$ost people who enjoy the good fortune of earning decently or above average are usually prone to unbridled taste; how much more someone earning outrageous amounts. Their confidence in their money quickly swells and so they believe all their desires can and should be met.

One of the biggest threats to sound financial health is when your unguarded desires are allowed to preponderate[37] over careful planning. What this results in is a situation where you start spending more than you're earning.

Many celebrities deliberately refuse to have their appetites tamed and reach to enjoy what they are not able to afford yet or would never be able to afford. However, because their public image offers them a bait, they heartily indulge themselves and are drawn into living on OPMs (Other People's Monies) which is only a nicer way to say living on debt.

They borrow money they don't have to buy luxury they don't need to impress a public whose loyalty is fickle[38]. This gives them the opportunity to spend more than they earn and invariably live beyond their means.

—————————————— DICTIONARY

37 Preponderate: Weigh more heavily
38 Fickle: Marked by erratic changeableness in affections or attachments

Like most other men driven by sight and materialism, the temptation to compete through acquisition weights on them and they succumb with little or no resistance. Exotic cars and mansions in exclusive parts of highbrow cities are part of the major capital spending that plunge celebrities into the undesirable position of living beyond their means.

The devil is more in the maintenance costs that accompany most of these capital acquisitions which is hardly considered at the point of acquiring. This is why many celebrities are in over their heads[39] financially.

In 1987, Michael Jackson bought his Neverland ranch for almost $20million. He spent another $35million improving the property which featured two railway lines, two helicopter pads, its own fire department, a zoo and a plethora of amusement park-style rides. What turned out to be financially crippling in the purchase was that he would be spending $10million annually to maintain it (he obviously did not consider this when purchasing the property).

In 2007, he was $23 million delinquent[40] on a $25 million loan he took out with the house. At a time, the zoo and many of the amusement park rides were auctioned off. Even more amazing is that he had been renting the Beverly Hills mansion where he lived.

---------------------- DICTIONARY

39 In over one's head: Having more difficulties than one can manage
40 Delinquent: Past due; not paid at the scheduled time

CELEBRITY SPOTLIGHT

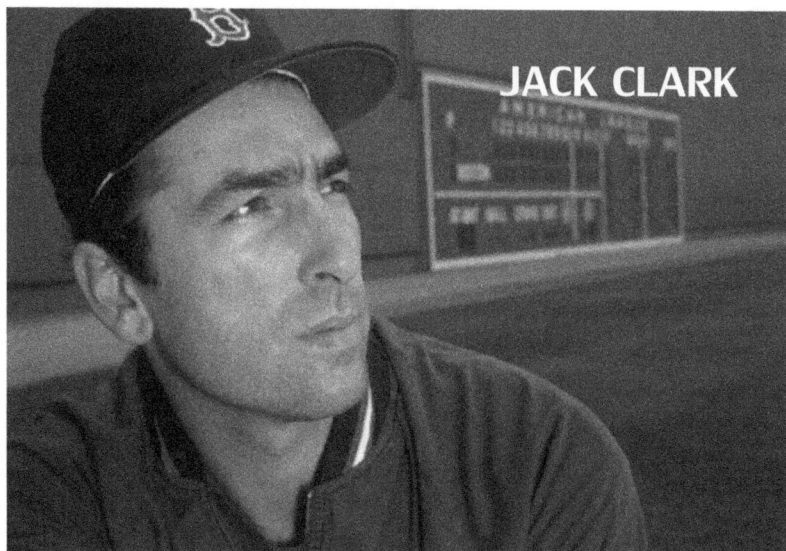

JACK CLARK

Jack Clark played for several baseball teams between 1975 and 1992. Also known as "Jack the Ripper," he played for the *San Francisco Giants, the St. Louis Cardinals, the New York Yankees, the San Diego Padres* and *the Boston Red Sox.*

However, in 1992, during his second year with the Sox, he declared bankruptcy, listing debts of almost $7 million. Clark was driven into bankruptcy in 1992 by his appetite for luxury cars.

When Clark listed his assets in the filing, he cited 18 luxury cars, including a $700,000 Ferrari, a Rolls Royce and a Mercedes Benz. He owed money on all but one of them. Apparently, Clark quickly got bored with his collection, and when that happened he would just get rid of the ones he no longer cared for and replace them with new ones. The habit ended up costing him his 2.4 million-dollar home and his drag-racing business because of his extravagant spending habits.

What you can do differently

*I*f you do not want to live beyond your means, you should ensure that your expenses are determined by your income so that you wouldn't be spending more than you can afford. Living beyond your means is a particularly risky strategy especially during volatile economic times.

No matter how much or how little you're paid or get from your work, you'll never get ahead if you spend more than you earn. Often it is easier to spend less than it is to earn more, and a little cost-cutting effort in a number of areas can result in big savings. It doesn't always have to involve making big sacrifices.

You should become more savvy[41] especially with shopping; do not let your emotion do the spending, be in charge of your money. Become less concerned about showing off or staying in vogue. Avoid situations that trigger your emotion to spend uncontrollably.

Have someone who would check your spending habits and can help ensure you're taking charge. It could be your spouse, your manager, your accountant, a relative etc. but be sure it's not someone who's got slippery fingers too.

Divorce yourself from the thought that there's a celebrity

———————————— DICTIONARY

41 Savvy: Shrewd and well informed

lifestyle pattern you must live to.

Take time to consider for how long you can maintain your current standard of living (bills, food, family expenses, mortgage, education, memberships etc) if your earning reduces or were to stop. If you cannot sustain your living standard for six to eighteen months (which is a reasonable enough time to reopen a new source of income), then you are not doing something right. You are probably living beyond your means.

You should consider cutting some frivolities, send your children to less expensive schools, drop membership of some clubs, reduce mortgage costs by moving to a less expensive apartment, drive a more fuel efficient car and so forth.

Make a budget and use it! It is a real eye opener to see where your money goes. Do not go for anything that cannot be accommodated by your budget. Even when you can afford it, ask yourself if your income can sustain it. Before changing your car, ask yourself if what you'd have left will be enough to maintain it.

Also, abhor[42] the philosophy that you will continue to earn from trading your skill and so you should keep spending.

——————————— DICTIONARY

42 Abhor: Find repugnant, detest

PITFALL 3

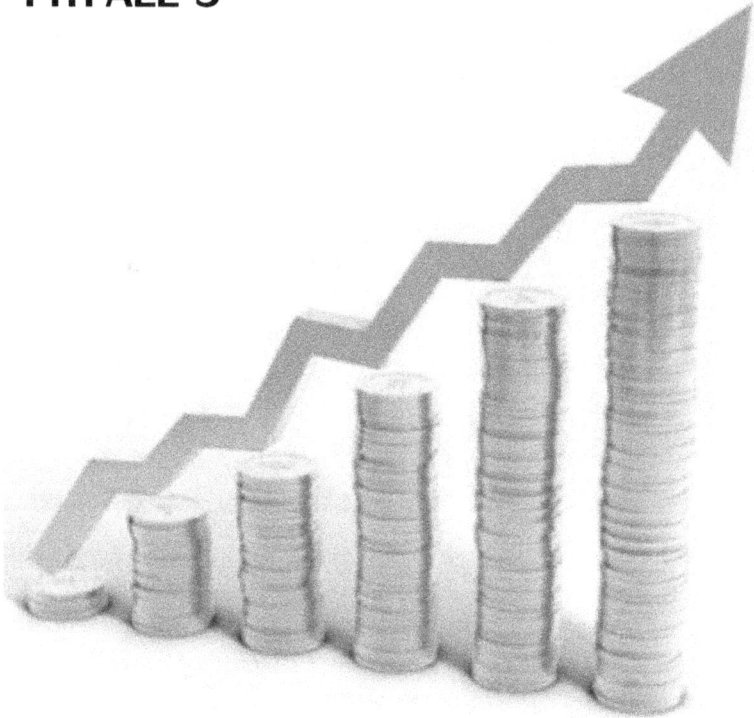

THEY DO NOT INVEST

CELEBRITY SPOTLIGHT

MEAT LOAF

Marvin Lee Aday better known as the singer Meat Loaf is an American rock musician and actor. He is noted for his 1977 album *Bat Out of Hell trilogy* consisting of *Bat Out of Hell, Bat Out of Hell II: Back Into Hell* and *Bat Out of Hell III: The Monster Is Loose. Bat Out of Hell* has sold more than 43 million copies. After more than 30 years, it still sells an estimated 200,000 copies annually, and stayed on the charts for over nine years. *Bat Out of Hell,* is one of the highest-selling of all time. Known for such classic songs as *"Two Out of Three Ain't Bad"* and *"Paradise by the Dashboard Light,"* the album made the singer a major, if unlikely, star. He earned a Grammy Award for Best Rock Vocal Performance Solo for a track on the latter album.

While attempting to create a follow-up to the huge hit album, he lost his voice and wasn't able to complete the recording until 1981, by which time he was no longer popular. The album that he recorded, *Dead Ringer*, sold only a tiny fraction of the amount that its predecessor sold, and by 1983 he was $1.6 million in debt, forcing him to declare bankruptcy.

*T*he best time in the life of a celebrity is that period when he's in high demand, earning his best, at peace with the media and in the good books of critics.

This period however, is also the period of undoing for many of them because at such times their imagination makes no suggestion to them that peak periods most certainly come to an end. They are so engrossed in this euphoria that they take little thought of the future.

No hot cake celebrity would ever think that things could stop being the way they are, that he could fall apart with his endorsers, have a protracted injury, stop being the fans favorite or even cease to be priced as exorbitantly as currently is.

Hardly would they think of investing in other ventures within or outside their area of career interest which would act as an alternative source of revenue. The excuses are usually the need to focus on their careers and work hard to make it to the peak. So it is almost impossible for them to even think of having to manage another venture either actively or passively.

The entertainment industry is a particularly demanding field of endeavor or so it seems; the higher they earn the more demanding managers, promoters, endorsers, fans, friends, family get. One of the members of the famous *spice girls* musical group implied once that their managers cared less about them as individuals and were unbearably exacting[43].

Even when one member of the group was ill, managers still felt their scheduled tours had to be met. With managers constantly hustling[44] them, nerve-wracking[45] schedules to meet, cut-throat[46] competition to beat and insatiable fans to please, many celebrities cannot help but be buried in their careers.

So, either by ignorance or deliberate indifference, they attempt no other source of income other than the big bucks they earn in salaries, intellectual property sales or endorsements. The usual slogan being - work hard, earn big, party hard.

Investing is an almost alien term in the circle of celebrities and those who actually invest are usually just going through the motions[47]. In the event that anything goes wrong with their careers they find nothing to fall back on. The route to bankruptcy is unencumbered[48] thence.

───────────────── DICTIONARY

43 Exacting: Severe and unremitting in making demands
44 Hustle: Pressure or urge someone into an action
45 Nerve-wracking: Stressful, causing great anxiety or distress
46 Cutthroat: Ruthless in competition
47 Going through the motions: To do something without believing it is important
48 Unencumbered: Free of obstruction

CELEBRITY SPOTLIGHT

MICHAEL VICK

Michael Dwayne Vick is an American football quarterback for the *Philadelphia Eagles* of the National Football League. He is almost as well known for his activities off the field as he is for his achievements on it. Prior to joining the Eagles, he played for the *Atlanta Falcons*, who had signed him to a record $62 million six-year contract, as well as a $3 million signing bonus. Then, three years later, he signed a ten-year extension worth $130 million, making him the highest-paid player in the NFL.

Everything seemed to be smooth sailing for Michael Vick until he went to prison for his participation in an illegal interstate dog fighting ring in 2007.

The prison sentence sidelined him for almost two years, and during that time he lost his regular NFL salary and all of his endorsements, including a lucrative Nike sponsorship. The lack of income, combined with his own financial mismanagement, forced Vick to declare bankruptcy from federal prison.

What you should do

*U*nderstand that financial security does not end with earning money. As stated earlier in this book, earning large has never been a guarantee of financial survival. There are more things you should do with your money before heading to paint the town red. One of such is INVEST.

Sound financial practice suggests that you carefully build your store of wealth with a deliberate intention to secure your financial future before taking on larger financial responsibilities.

Robert G. Allen in his book, *Multiple Streams of Income* stated that: *"Today, very few families can survive on less than two streams of income. In the volatile future, you will need a portfolio of income streams - not one or two - but many streams from completely different and diversified sources."*

In George Clason's 1926 personal finance classic, *the richest man in Babylon*, Babylon's wealthiest man Arkad suggested seven cures to a lean purse to the have-nots of Babylon who had come to learn the laws of wealth at his feet. *'Make thy gold multiply'* was the third cure.

"The gold we may retain from our earnings is but the start. The earnings it will make shall build our fortunes". The process of multiplying your earning or expanding your sources of income is INVESTING.

Investing is a good way to diversify your earning and income source. Investing helps to shift your current residual purchasing power from high earning periods to low earning periods, in the process securing for you a future income. When well executed, it serves a very good cushion in times of distress and industry or economic downturns.

Nigerian billionaire industrialist, Chief Rasaq Okoya, recounted in a 2004 interview how investing in real estate became a hedge when his manufacturing business was not performing optimally.

"Manufacturing is a very sensitive business. It has an on-and-off season. That is one of the reasons we are into different lines of manufacturing business. When any line of product is in the low cycle, you need to have other avenues to make up."

He further stated, *"The area we have invested heavily is in property business. These properties are our hedge against the fluctuations in manufacturing industry. We collect millions of Naira rent from these properties, which sustain us during the period of downturns in manufacturing industry."*

Seek viable alternative sources of generating income for yourself. There are countless businesses you can venture a try.

But before you take the plunge[49] ensure you do your due diligence[50] thoroughly.

Take time to go through all the options you have, decide what kind of business you would want to be associated with or inclined to. Look at the people involved in relation to their capacity to manage the venture profitably well, measure their track records and experience considering carefully how it aligns with the proposed business.

Also find out how much of their own fund is or will be involved. Be careful to take up all the risk since you would not be managing it yourself or is not going to be managed by someone you can vouch for without reservation.

You can also invest in existing businesses you find fascinating. However, ensure you take a critical look at the state of health of the business. If you do not have a good knowledge of business analysis, employing the services of a good analyst will do you a lot of good here. Some businesses are actually just façades[See 29].

Aside investing in real business ventures, financial assets are also good sources of earning residual or passive income.

DICTIONARY

49 Plunge: to become involved in something with great enthusiasm
50 Due diligence: The degree of care that a prudent person would exercise, which is a legally relevant standard for establishing liability.

Financial assets are claims on the returns or income of real assets. They are called "Securities". Invariably, financial assets are dependent on the income of real assets for their own profitability.

Shares and Bonds are examples of financial assets since their profit structure is wrapped around the assets of a real business or other institutions. Examples include; shares, bonds, debentures, investment trusts, mutual funds etc.
Other investment options include real estate, commodities and Foreign Exchange (FOREX) trading.

Before staking your money into any of these, ensure you are well informed about what you're investing in.

PITFALL 4

THEY INVEST WITHOUT KNOWLEDGE

CELEBRITY SPOTLIGHT

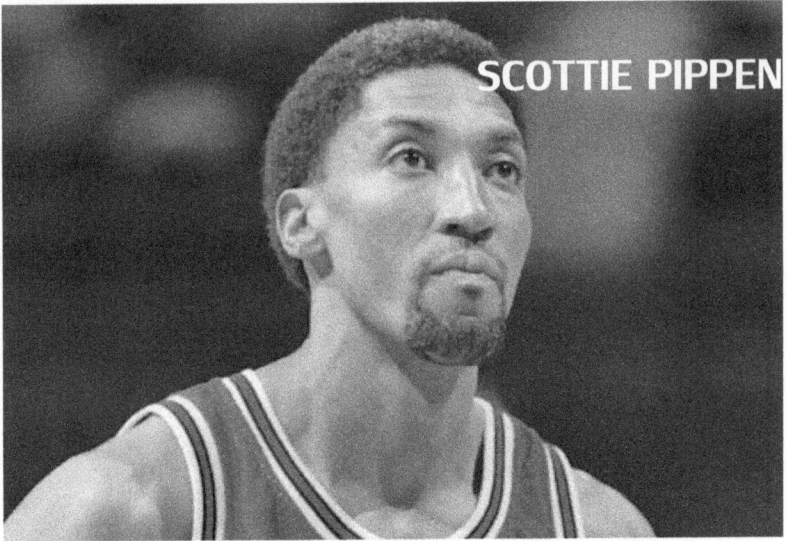

SCOTTIE PIPPEN

Scottie Maurice Pippen is a retired American professional basketball player who played in the National Basketball Association (NBA). He is most remembered for his time with the *Chicago Bulls*, with whom he was instrumental in six NBA Championships and their record 1995/96 season of 72 wins. Considered one of the best small forwards of all time, He was named one of the 50 Greatest Players in NBA History during the 1996/97 season, and is one of four players to have his jersey retired by the Chicago Bulls. Pippen is also the only person to have twice won both an NBA championship and an Olympic gold medal in the same year. Pippen was inducted into the Basketball Hall of Fame on August 13, 2010.

According to *Investopedia*, since retirement Pippen has lost $120 million in career earnings because of poor financial planning and bad business deals. He blew $27 million on bad investments and spent $4.3 million on a Gulfstream II corporate jet that was grounded just months after he bought it.

*C*elebrities (sports stars, musicians, comedians and other entertainers) hardly invest; when they do, it is more often than not suicidal rather than beneficial. Investing is a way to put your money to work so as to earn you more wealth – wealth you did not actively participate in earning. So investing is generally a good engagement. However, when investing is done without the requisite knowledge, it becomes highly risky and damning to financial prosperity.

Many celebrities, owing to the sudden windfall they get, are bombarded with a deluge[51] of business proposals from friends, family and even unrelated jobbers[52]. Everyone seems to have a business idea that will make phenomenal profit and they (the celebrities) are always the person in the best position to provide venture funding because they *'got the dough'*.

In naivety[53], believing that their interest is what is uppermost in the mind of the proposing partners, they venture without having the slightest knowledge of what the venture is about or how it'll serve their best financial interest.

Most times, what is principal in their minds is the proposed profit that the business will rake in. Little or no attention is given to investigating whether or not the business has the capacity to generate such income. And since their bank

---

DICTIONARY

51 Deluge: An overwhelming number or amount
52 Jobber: Somebody who does piecework or work on a job by job basis
53 Naivety: Deficient in relevant experience

accounts have funds lying close to idle, they invest – which in this light is actually just another way to spend frivolously and without wisdom.

American actress and former fashion model Kim Basinger bought the small town of Braselton, Georgia in 1989 for US$20 million, to establish as a tourist attraction with movie studios and film festival after some family member recommended same to her. She met financial difficulties and sold it in 1993. In a 1998 interview with Barbara Walters Basinger admitted that "nothing good came out of it" because a rift resulted within her family.

It has often been said that, you put your money where your mouth is. This statement, to a large extent, is true if the *'mouth'* is rightly taken to represent the store of knowledge. So to paraphrase this, *'put your money where your knowledge is'* or better still *'don't put your money where your knowledge is not'*.

Best selling author, Robert Kiyosaki emphasized this when he wrote, *'to put your money where your knowledge is not is financial suicide'* – celebrities are experts at this.

Many bankrupt celebrities are the forlorn[54] victims of various failed business ventures which they invested in without an

--------------------------- DICTIONARY

54 Forlorn: hopeless; desperate and doomed to failure

inkling of knowledge.

Former US Senator, author and businessman George Mcgovern who had gone into the business world, as an hotelier, after his political career wrote in a 1992 edition of the Wall Street Journal; *"I wish that during the years I was in public office, I had had firsthand experience about the difficulties business people face every day"*. His Stratford Inn had gone bankrupt in 1991.

CELEBRITY SPOTLIGHT

JOHNNY UNITAS

John Constantine Unitas known as Johnny Unitas was as legendary a player as there is in the annals of NFL history . Nicknamed "The Golden Arm," his career spanned three decades and saw him set record after record, winning the Most Valuable Player award three times and throwing touchdown passes in 47 consecutive games, a record which still stands today. Off the field, however, it was another story.

The legendary quarterback had attempted to parlay his earnings into shrewd business moves, such as restaurants, real estate ventures and bowling alleys, but these endeavors never performed in the way that he had hoped. Ultimately, he declared bankruptcy in 1991.

What you can do differently

*T*he formula here is, 'do not put your money in what you do not have knowledge of or do not understand'. As much as possible, get at least the fundamental knowledge of anything you want to make an investment in.

No matter how seemingly lucrative, popular or low risk as any investment proposition may appear, make sure you garner some knowledge about it, enough to help you make a well informed decision to invest or not to invest; to invest big time or thread with caution.

In 2004, a research report from *China Economic Quarterly* (CEQ) revealed that many foreign businesses in China were struggling to make money at all. The reason was not farfetched; China is seen as a reservoir of untapped potential by foreign companies looking for new markets. With its billion-plus population and breakneck[55] economic growth, it was intuitively[56] a destination of choice.

However, many of these companies didn't take time to understand the peculiar cut-throat[See46] competition and incredibly challenging conditions of the local Chinese market. According to Dr Benoit Rossignol, an expert in foreign investment in the Chinese food and retail market,

––––––––––––––––– DICTIONARY

55 Breakneck: Moving at very high speed
56 Intuitive: Spontaneously derived from or prompted by a natural tendency

"Knowledge is the key to taking advantage of any lucrative market. We have seen Fortune 500 companies losing lots of money in China by over-investing, investing too quickly or too early and companies with less than $500,000 of investment being very successful within three to four years because they knew where to position themselves, and make the best use of their money".

Two basic things you should do to increase your knowledge is *word up* and *stuff up*.

Word up: every sector has its peculiar language so word up by doing some research and understand the lingo used in your chosen investment option. If you do not understand the language, how will you keep up with developments, incoming news etc. Just like there are medical terms, legal terms, equity investing terms etc. so there are terms wherever it is you intend to put your money. Learn it!

Stuff up: know the operations, processes, procedures and happenings in your choice of investment. To stuff up you need hindsight – a bit of history, Insight – the current state of the industry and foresight – have a glimpse of what the future holds.

All these can be achieved by reading; there is virtually nothing that something has not been written about. You can listen to tapes, watch videos, attend courses etc. if you do all these diligently, you would garner enough knowledge to take at least a step at actual interaction with the investment system.

Also, employ the services of professionals and consultants before, during and after you invest. You obviously will be more engaged with your job so employing professionals where it is necessary will help you keep an extra eye on your investments.

Not just any professional but trustworthy and competent professionals. Lawyers, investment managers, real estate professionals etc. have expertise in seeing the demerits of many business plans and investment proposals you would be receiving.

According to *BusinessInsider,* the majority of famous athletes making poor business decisions often stem from their associations with non-investment professionals such as family members, friends and the always mysterious "advisors."

A former corporate promotions manager at Globacom Nigeria once recounted that of all the artists (musicians, comedians, sports stars, actors and actresses) that the company had signed endorsement deals with in about seven years, only one (a footballer) came with a lawyer to negotiation and contract signing sessions.

Assume there had been unfavorable clauses in the contract;

do you think they would have known? See page 75 for tips on *'how not to invest'*.

PITFALL 5

THEY DO NOT PROTECT
THEIR INCOME

CELEBRITY SPOTLIGHT

TONY BRAXTON

www.tvfunspot.com

Toni Braxton is an American R&B singer, songwriter and actress. Braxton has won six Grammy Awards, seven American Music Awards, and five Billboard Music Awards and has sold over 60 million records worldwide. Braxton topped the Billboard 200 with her 1993 self-titled debut album and continued that streak with her second studio album *Secrets*, which spawned the number-one hits *"You're Makin' Me High"* and *"Un-Break My Heart"*. Although she had successful albums and singles, Braxton shortly filed for bankruptcy after racking up a $20,000 American Express bill and monthly expenses of over $43,000, but then returned with her chart-topping third album, *The Heat*.

Braxton's career renaissance was so successful that she was asked to headline the Flamingo Hotel in Las Vegas in 2006. The show proved so popular that its run was extended through 2008. However, On April 8, 2008, near the end of her two-year run at the Flamingo Hotel, Braxton was briefly hospitalized and the remaining dates on the show, which was scheduled to end on August 23, 2008, were canceled, but the cancellation incurred debts in the tens of millions of dollars. Braxton filed for bankruptcy a second time in October 2010.

*P*retty Joe (not real name) was a fast rising standup comedian in Nigeria. His career had picked up on the fast lane after he won the AY open Mic Comedy challenge. With a string of shows to perform at and the monetary gratification that comes with it, a new car was inevitable to own, and he acquired one.

Four short years into his professional career however, he arrived the *TymeOut Lounge* in Lagos where he had joined his colleagues for a session where consultants trained young comedians on evolving world class brands, in public transport. The reason: He had lost his car to robbers a few months after he acquired it. His solace was in the fact that he would soon buy another one an obvious financial setback for him.

This sort of incident, for the comic industry, was just 'as usual'; for them, he had just joined a growing long list of victims.

A few months before his first album (superstar) launch, new music act whiz kid also lost his car to armed men. He was just another recurrent decimal in the music industry too.

When many footballers and sport stars with citizenship in the third world arrive from their career bases in Europe and America, they are often times victims of robberies and they lose valuables in the process.

The solution, unlike what whiz kid said to an entertainment reporter after his incident, is not to triple security. What about if the loss was due to accident, theft of a static vehicle, loss due to fire etc?

The incidences of loss to unanticipated incidents are everyday experiences in most societies; counter preventive measures may not necessarily be the way to go in some of these cases. Considering personal finance, when these incidents occur the question becomes, who bears the financial burden of replacing lost property?

This is where many celebrities are found wanting in that they do not protect their assets by insuring them so that when such accidents happen, the insurance company takes up the cost of redemption.

As it is common with many who lack financial aptitude, insurance is alien and in most cases seen as betting on odds or a sign of faithlessness in the divine. They therefore take themselves through the torture of saving all over again to acquire another car or any other valuable they have lost, drawing perilously[57] from already strained finances.

The implication of this ignorance is that, when celebrities who spend a larger chunk of their money acquiring all sorts of

―――――――――――― DICTIONARY

57 Perilously: In a dangerous manner

expensive goods for themselves fail to protect it, they are faced with a huge financially devastating burden of replacing them if they lose it. Added to that is that they may not even have completed paying for this expensive properties before they lose them.

Aside the loss of property, celebrities like every other member of the society who is human are a t the risk of health setbacks which could also be financially damaging and many do not have insurance protection for this very important part of their lives.

A national study by Harvard and Ohio University, published in *The American Journal of Medicine*, showed that the leading cause of bankruptcy in the United States is due to unpaid medical bills. Over 60% of all 2007 bankruptcy filings were connected to unaffordable medical and hospital expenses.

With the risk of any form of loss not obliterated[58], the imminence of a financial disaster persists where insurance is not appreciated.

——————————— DICTIONARY

58 Obliterate: Remove completely from recognition or memory

CELEBRITY SPOTLIGHT

ZSA ZSA GABOR

Zsa Zsa Gabor is a Hungarian-born American stage, film and television actress. She acted on stage in Vienna, Austria, in 1932, and was crowned Miss Hungary in 1936. She emigrated to the United States in 1941 and became a sought-after actress with "European flair and style", with a personality that "exuded charm and grace".

In 2002, Gabor was a passenger in an automobile crash, partially paralyzed, and was hospitalized for several weeks. In 2005, she suffered a stroke, underwent surgery to remove an arterial blockage, and returned home a few weeks later. In 2007, she had surgery related to her previous stroke, and then underwent surgery to treat an infection. In July 2010, Gabor was taken to the hospital after she fell at home, requiring hip replacement.

In January 2011 the *Los Angeles Times* reported that Zsa Zsa Gabor was being forced to sell her $28 million home in order to pay her medical bills because she had no health insurance besides Medicare. According to her husband *"She partied with the rich and famous, flirted and sometimes got married, but she did not think of the future."*

50

What you should do differently

*T*he risk of loss or damage to property (including automobiles, jewelry, real estate, personal effects, tech equipments and health) is an ever present one. It therefore behooves[59] on you to ensure that all your valuables are adequately insured.

You should get an insurance policy for all your valuables. Buying insurance is simply putting a price on peace of mind or buying what you do not intend to need. With insurance, you secure redemption for the insured property in advance of an untoward eventuality.

Always include the cost of paying insurance premium in your budget as part of your expenses. Insurance offers a good hedge for your finances in that you are assured of replacement of any insured property you lose or is damaged. The premium you will pay is way below what it would cost you to replace such property in the event of a loss.

Draw an auto-insurance policy for your car, preferably comprehensive insurance as against the legally mandated third party insurance. With a comprehensive insurance coverage, your insurer will take up all cost of repairs in the event of damage due to a collision and would replace the car

———————————— DICTIONARY

59 Behooves: Be appropriate or necessary

with a new one in the case of theft. Third party insurance on the other hand only protects a third party i.e. someone or another car that is injured or damaged in an accident where you are found to be the cause. With a comprehensive coverage, you wouldn't have to take yourself through the torture of saving all over again to acquire another one each time you lose your car or get it damaged.

Insure your house and its contents against fire, theft or damage due to weather or burglary. Have your health insured too so you get high quality treatment anytime you fall ill without bearing the burden of the bills. If you have to fund the redemption of every valuable property you lose, it could be financially perilous.

Do not flow with the opinion that paying insurance premium is simply dashing out money to the insurer. It isn't so. You're actually purchasing for yourself peace of mind and more financial security. There's no swifter way for money to fly off your pocket than a property lost without insurance.

PITFALL 6

THEY ACQUIRE
LIABILITIES

CELEBRITY SPOTLIGHT

MC HAMMER

MC Hammer (real name: Stanley Kirk Burrell) is an American rapper, entertainer, business entrepreneur, dancer and actor. He had his greatest commercial success and popularity from the late 1980s until the mid-1990s. Remembered for a rapid rise to fame before losing the majority of his fortune, Hammer is also known for his hit records, including "U Can't Touch This", flamboyant dance movements and trademark Hammer pants. Hammer's superstar-status made him a household name and pop icon. He has sold more than 50 million records worldwide.

Sadly, his fame didn't last, and before he knew it, he was $13.7 million in debt with only $9.6 million in assets, prompting him to file for bankruptcy in 1996 as a result of the fickle public growing bored with his positive and poppy style during the rise of gangsta rap, as well as excessive spending while supporting friends and family.

Hammer had amassed approximately US$33 million. US$12 million of this total was used to have his Xanadu-like home built in Fremont, California. Jet magazine estimated that Hammer employed 200 people, with an annual payroll of US$6.8 million. The mansion was sold for a fraction of its former price.

*T*his is a direct product of the point discussed earlier that celebrities live beyond their means. Their unrestrained capital spending is what plunges them into debt. Worse still are the chains of expenses that these acquisitions bring with them in form of maintenance costs. The many properties and toys or other 'trappings of wealth' celebrities spend their money to acquire are in the intrinsic[60] sense liabilities that create holes in their pockets. According to the *Sage of Omaha* and the world's greatest investor, Warren Buffet, he sees the maintenance cost and expense associated with these things as a burden.

In simple terms, a liability is whatever creates an obligation to pay money to another party. The amount used in buying personal possessions is not in itself the major problem but the residual expenses it plunges the acquirer into by opening a consistent 'money loss channel' in their finances.

Many celebrities quickly acquire liabilities as soon as they earn a windfall because all they think they are losing is the capital they are spending on the product. They give very little or no consideration to the cost of maintaining it nor bounce these maintenance costs against their earning.

Houses in high end parts of the city, luxury cars and exclusive club memberships form the bulk of the liabilities artists and

---
DICTIONARY

60 Intrinsic: Belonging to a thing by its very nature

sport stars acquire.

Many of them also tend to keep multiple residences they hardly stay in; they stock their garages with cars they mostly simply acquire for the sake of collection and the pride of ownership. Because of the naturally materialistic nature of carnal man, celebrities tend to always want to compete on the grounds of material acquisition and spend instantly on things that impress their new millionaire statuses. This emotional inclination causes them to spend with instant gratification in mind falling into the trap and weight of liabilities.

Owning private jets, helicopters, sport cars and highbrow real estate before even acquiring an income generating asset or before creating other streams of income is willingly signing your bankruptcy papers before actually becoming bankrupt.

For many celebrities, most of these properties were on the long run sold off to pay the debt they (the liabilities) generated [refer to the Michael Jackson story on page 20].

Another form of liability that has created holes in many celebrity pockets (especially male) is women. Many male celebrities are in multiple male-female relationships. The financial implication of these relationships (many times illicit) could be monumental. As singles, they would be compelled to gratify the financial appetite of all these girlfriends.

They buy cars and other gifts for each new girl, dinners and night-outs, hotel bills and the list goes on. One thing leads to another and they now have children they did not intend for. Then they have to pay rent/mortgage for multiple apartments, school fees, child support etc.

Also crippling is the cost they incur with their multiple divorces which you can bet on that their marriages will always result to. Comedian Eddy Griffin for example has been married twice, has four baby mamas and is father to nine children. Nigerian singer-songwriter, 2face Idibia is reported to have five children from three baby mamas.

CELEBRITY SPOTLIGHT

KENNY ANDERSON

Kenny Anderson is a retired American basketball player. He earned an estimated $60 million during his NBA career after playing for nine different teams.

He was married three times, and the divorce from his first wife, Tami Akbar, had cost him dearly. She successfully challenged their prenuptial agreement and walked away with half his assets and $8,500 a month in child support. To celebrate her court victory, she had a custom license plate made that read "HISCASH."

In addition to monthly child support and alimony payments to Akbar, Anderson was also supporting six other children and two other ex-wives, as well as making monthly payments on his mother's house. He also owned eight cars and an estate in Beverly Hills, and gave himself a $10,000-a-month allowance that he referred to as "hanging out money". At the time of his bankruptcy filing, he had $41,000 in monthly expenses to pay.

What you should do differently

*W*hen you earn a windfall or accumulate some money in savings, the first thing is to consider how you can perpetuate your earning stream and grow it well beyond your expenses.

To do this, you should acquire and/or buy assets and not liabilities. An asset is something that generates income for you beyond what you spend on maintaining it. You must as much as possible live below your means while you set up more income streams that are independent of your active participation. A non-systemized income source is at the greater risk of extinction than a systemized income source.

Your expenses on your basic needs such as shelter, clothing and feeding should be kept moderate and unostentatious[61] until you open more income streams. Ensure you derive maximum value from every penny you spend.

It will also do you a lot of good to be sexually disciplined and abstain from committing yourself to numerous relationships with the opposite sex. Take counsel on how to choose the right marriage partner instead of flowing with your emotion (which is only temporal). This is to avoid unnecessary divorce and the concomitant expenses that come with it.

--------------- DICTIONARY

61 Unostentatious: Exhibiting restrained good taste

Comedian Eddie griffin married his first wife at the age of 15 and divorced her one year later].

Beware of financial predators; people who depend on you for stipends and offer no value to you in return.

They usually come in the form of hangers-on such as jobless family members, old friends etc. If you have to support family members, ensure it is to the tune that can be accommodated by your budget while encouraging them to also seek independence. You can keep a stipendiary[62] account to track how much this gesture is taking out of you.

Be quick to recognize any thing that is constantly taking more money from you than you deem relevant and exhibit restraint immediately.

DICTIONARY

62 Stipendiary: Pertaining to or of the nature of a stipend or allowance

FINANCIAL PLANNING
TIPS

CELEBRITY SPOTLIGHT

SINBAD

David Atkins aka Sinbad is an American stand-up comedian and actor. He became well known in the 1990s from being featured on his own HBO specials, appearing on several television series. By the early 1990s, his popularity had grown enough for Fox to green-light The Sinbad Show, which premiered September 16, 1993. In 2004 he was named the #78 greatest stand-up comic of all time on "Comedy Central Presents: 100 Greatest Stand-Ups of All Time".

In 2009, Sinbad was placed in the top 10 of the 250 worst tax debtors for the state of California. The comedian owed the State $2.5 million in personal income tax. On December 11, 2009, Sinbad filed for bankruptcy for bad debts of $8.15 million. The actor claimed that he has only $50,000 in assets and $10-$50 million in liabilities. On February 5, 2010, it was reported that Sinbad put up his 2.5-acre (10,000 m²) hilltop home for sale in order to alleviate his tax burdens.

*T*he thrust of success in life and in most endeavors is planning; a prosperous financial future is not an exception. We have produced here a list of tips you can employ in your financial planning.

Have a saving plan

You've probably heard it before: Pay yourself first! It's the oldest financial tip in the book. If you wait until you've met all your other financial obligations before seeing what's left over for saving, chances are you will never have a healthy savings account or investments.

Resolve to set aside a minimum of 5% to 10% of your salary for savings BEFORE you start paying your bills. Better yet, have money automatically deducted from your paycheck and deposited into a separate account.

Contribute to a retirement plan

Whether you are starting off your career at 17 or have reached your peak at 23 or preparing to leave the scene at 32, you should always set your eyes on securing yourself financially for the day when you would not be able to work or when certain conditions barricade your capacity to earn.

Contribute to a retirement plan and build up wealth for your future. When in the hands of a good manager, you can be rest assured that your contributions will keep growing geometrically.

If not for any other reason consider the embarrassing state of many old and impoverished hit-makers of the past who now support themselves with stipends from charitable friends.

Stick with a Budget

Once you have your savings and retirement contributions safely stashed, you then decide how the rest would be spent among your many desire. Budgeting then sets in.

Budgeting is a simple core financial principle that's all about knowing how much you have left to spend and how much you're expected to pay out and matching the two together. How can you know where your money is going if you don't budget? How can you set spending and saving goals if you don't know where your money is going?

You need a budget whether you make million or hundreds of thousands of naira a year. Some celebrities would usually say, 'budgeting is for people who do not make enough money.' The many scenarios in this book definitely suggest otherwise.

Budgeting helps you to be frugal. Frugality is not being miserly like it is usually wrongly affirmed, it is simply about learning to spend the money you have on wise purchases and informed choices that won't get you into financial trouble later. Make sure your budget does not exceed what you have to spend; keep your desires within your funds.

Spend wisely

How you use the money available for you to spend is one very important part of your financial life. Always spend wisely, go for quality but not ostentatious goods. When you buy quality products you get maximum value, it lasts longer and you can easily trade it in if you need a new one.

Avoid spending impulsively or at a whim[63]. Do not be tempted to buy sub-standard products because they're cheaper; they would usually not offer commensurate[64] value and quickly turn into a waste of resources.

Be disciplined in your spending by sticking to your budget. No matter how much you have, how you spend your money makes the difference.

———————————— DICTIONARY

63 Whim: a sudden thought or desire, based on impulse rather than reason or necessity
64 Commensurate: Corresponding in size, degree or extent

Pay off debt & guard against debt

Borrowing especially for consumption is deadly to your financial success. Keep your debt low or do not borrow at all. Before you do, ensure you can cater for it in the short term. As at the time of filing for bankruptcy in March 2010, former *New Jersey Nets* player Derrick Coleman had debts totaling more than $4 million, which he owed to almost 100 creditors.

Do not go into debt to finance consumption like food, clothing or throwing a party. They're never worth it in the end.

Invest

If you're contributing to a retirement plan and a savings account and you can still manage to put some money into other investments, all the better. Investments offer a source of earning residual income.

Because of the technicality of businesses, it is important that you very well understand INVESTING as a financial concept. The next section of this book is wholly dedicated to helping you understand the concept of investing.

Steer clear of credit shopping

You may have heard the saying, "credit makes the world go round" but credit can also spin the world out of balance; how much more you. "Don't spend money you don't have but think you might acquire in the future." Be mindful about saving and thoughtful about spending, says Susan Hirshman, author of *"Does This Make My Assets Look Fat?."*

Former *Carolina Panthers* star wideout, Muhsin Muhammad was once sued by Wachovia for $25,000 in credit card debt. You don't want to be in his shoes.

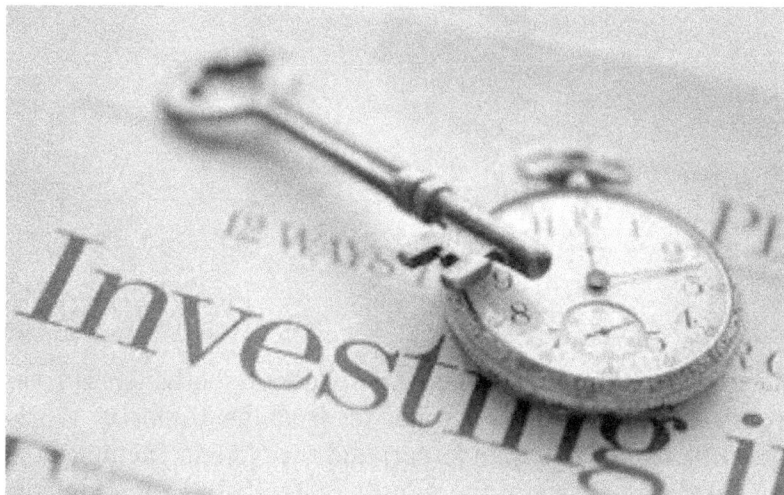

WHAT INVESTING
IS

CELEBRITY SPOTLIGHT

CELESTINE BABAYARO

Celestine Babayaro is a former Nigerian footballer. He was part of the victorious Nigerian team at the Under-17 World Championships in Japan (1993) and the Nigeria Olympic gold medal winning team at the Atlanta 96 football event and made the tournament's all-star team having scored in the Gold Medal game itself against Argentina.

He moved to Belgium club Anderlecht in 1994 and played for Chelsea (1997), Newcastle (2005) and Los Angeles Galaxy (2008) before officially announcing his retirement from football on 8 July 2010. Babayaro was named Belgian Young Footballer of the Year 1995 & 1996 while playing for Anderlecht. During his time at Chelsea, the team won the FA Cup and Charity Shield in 2000, and reached the FA Cup final in 2002.

Babayaro was signed by Chelsea in April 1997 moving for a transfer fee of £2.25 million, a club record paid for a teenager at the time. He was signed for Newcastle United for £1m in 2005. At one stage in his career, the ex-Nigerian international was reported to earn £25,000-a-week. Early 2011, his neighbors said they feared he had fallen on hard times because the upkeep of his £475,000 property in Shepperton, Middlesex had slipped. He was declared bankrupt on 9 February 2011.

INVESTING DEFINED
Culled from Investing according to Stakes by Stakes

*W*hile putting all other definitions into perspective, we would expound on investing thus: "Investing is the commitment of a resource on an asset over a period with the expectation of returns in any form especially capital growth". This definition contains the key terms that make an action fit to be called an investment. These terms are explained in more detail:

Resource: this is the present pleasure sacrificed for the expected future income or capital growth. It is a popular notion that nothing goes for nothing, meaning you can't make money or gain anything without first giving something, *"nothing ventured, nothing gained"*.

Look at this like a farmer with an edible seed; instead of enjoying the savor of the seed as food, he decides to plant it in expectation of a return of a field of food. Not eating the seed is a sacrifice, on his part, of a present pleasure he could have derived from eating the seed. The seed therefore is a resource.

Most times, in tangible terms, the resource is money. Another resource, though intangible, is 'time' presumed to be man's most valuable resource.

Asset: assets describe something, in which you commit your resource, that has the capacity to generate returns. In the case of the farmer described above, the land into which the farmer puts his seed is an asset because it has the capacity to reproduce the seed in multiple folds.

Anything that does not have the capacity to generate returns, in one form or another, cannot be considered an asset. But it is worthy to note, that the capacity to generate returns does not imply that the asset is armored from loss; loss is still possible after committing resource on an asset based on some other factors. We will discuss more on assets later in the book.

Period: this is the lapse (passing of time) between when you commit your resource into the asset and when you get your returns. In investing, there is always a time over which the asset will be allowed to 'brood on' the resource in order to produce the desired returns. It is impracticable to invest now and expect an instant return without a lapse - even if it is a second.

The period is not a fixed time but ranges from a few minutes to years (in some instances) depending on what asset you have put your resource into. You do not invest now and expect your returns immediately; you should learn to *"give time some time"*.

Returns: the extra you get after a period on the resource you invested in an asset is what is termed returns. See from the definition of investing given earlier that the return is an expectation and not a guaranteed earning. This means that the reason why you have invested is because you expect to get returns and not because returns always come out of every investment.

The returns could be in material form or in form of an improvement in skill depending on the asset invested in.

The above elucidation is the absolute and explicit description investing can get. Any action that falls within the jurisdiction of this explanation can be referred to as an investment. And any one that falls short, in any way, cannot be termed investing.

WHAT INVESTING
IS NOT

CELEBRITY SPOTLIGHT

ANTOINE WALKER

Antoine Walker is an American professional basketball player with the *Idaho Stampede* of the NBA Development League. He was drafted with the sixth overall pick in the 1996 NBA Draft out of the University of Kentucky and played in the NBA from 1996 – 2008. In a career lasting 15 years with five different NBA teams, he's collected one NBA championship and reportedly earned $110 million.

However, in May 2010, he filed for bankruptcy, claiming assets of $4 million and liabilities of almost $13 million. The filing listed four pieces of real estate including a $2.3 million Miami home that is underwater with a mortgage of $3.6 million.

Walker's problems stem in large part from gambling. Walker was arrested on July 15 2009 at *Harrah's Casino* in South Lake Tahoe, Nevada. The charges stemmed from over $800,000 in gambling debts and on June 30, 2010 he was arraigned for bad check charges for his failure to pay $770,000 in gambling losses to *Caesars Palace* and two other casinos in Las Vegas, Nevada.

A couple of years ago, the case was reported of an international businessman who after losing a couple of thousands of dollars <u>gambling</u> in a new Mexican casino was approached by reporters who asked about how he felt of his latest losses, he said, "in <u>investing</u>, you lose some and you win some".

Personal finance tutors have over the years popularized the concept of investing as a critical part and tool in the making of a financially exciting life. On the basis of the enormous benefits that it has been taught to provide, very many people have made many financial moves that have resulted in gains and also in losses. The losses have caused some victims to lose faith in the investment concept.

However, a closer look at the many instances where investors have suffered losses (the scenario above for example) shows that they were actually not investing. Losses have resulted mostly from a wrong perception and/or belief about what investing is. These wrong notions about investing are what we intend to expose here in order to make you a better informed investor.

But before we go on into what investing is not, let us redress a popular fallacy about investing which has found penetration into many investors' belief systems—that **'investing is based on chance'**.

This is an outright fallacy. Investing is not a game of chance as many teachers have made it appear. The truth is this; every investment move made may not result in a gain but that does not make investing a 'win some and lose some game'. You can predict, to a high degree, that your investment move will result in a gain if you understand and follow the proper guiding principles that guarantee profit.

Please note and don't get this wrong, an appreciation of the guiding principles does not debar the risk factor from investing. The risk as it is associated with investing is based on unforeseen and uncontrollable factors that may surface after the investment has been made. And since it is not for man to predict the future with absolute accuracy, the risk element cannot be exhumed from investing.

So, investing is not based on chance; just stick with that. It is possible to always be a winner as an investor; all you need is to understand...

WHAT INVESTING IS NOT

Investing is not:

1. Gambling: gambling as defined by the oxford advanced learners dictionary is the activity of playing games of chance for money and of betting on horses etc. Betting is the act of risking money or other resources on the unknown result of an event. Merging these two together implies that gambling is the activity of playing **games of chance** for money and **risking**

money etc. on the **unknown result** of an event e.g. a horse race.

Note the emphasized words in the definition above are contrary to those of investing and this makes gambling unworthy of being classified as an investment -

Chance: as explained earlier, investing is not a game based on chance.

Risking money: the risk element in this definition for gambling can obviously not be compared with that of investing; the risk here represents an enormous amount of intractable risk unlike investing where you can increase or decrease the level of risk in an investment move.

Unknown result: since in investing you can predict to high degrees that your investment move would result in a gain means gambling cannot be a form of investing.

2. Lottery/Lotto: governments and charity organizations sometimes sell tickets with numbers printed on them which people buy. The numbers are then picked by **chance** and the people with those numbers win prizes. The successes in this game are based on luck rather than on effort or careful organization, information or skill.

We have just paraphrased, above, various definitions for lottery and lotto given by renowned dictionaries. Again, look at the predominant words; **chance, luck**; this cannot be a form of investing since the results are plagued with uncertainty.

3. Speculation: twentieth century American billionaire and philanthropist, Andrew Carnegie, said in his 'Uses Of Wealth' while describing the steps to phenomenal riches that, *"...and it is his duty that he begins to save a portion of his earnings and invest them,* **not in speculation** *but securities or in property or in any legitimate business in such form as will..."* - our emphasis.

But what exactly is speculation you would like to ask. Speculation describes the act of guessing without knowing all the facts about something. It is the act of trying to make profits by speculating. In these definitions you will see that speculation is contrary to fact based analysis that is a critical principle for profitable investing because the facts are not even known talk less analyzing the facts and making a decision based on that.

Investing based on an invalid rumor is a popular form of speculation that investors engage in which you should avoid.

HOW NOT TO
INVEST

CELEBRITY SPOTLIGHT

KIM BASINGER

Kim Basinger is an American actress and former fashion model. She is known for her portrayals of Domino Petachi, the Bond girl in *Never Say Never Again* (1983), and Vicki Vale, the female lead in *Batman*(1989). Basinger received a Golden Globe Award for Best Supporting Actress– Motion Picture nomination for her work in *The Natural* (1984). She won an Academy Award, Golden Globe, and Screen Actors Guild Award for Best Supporting Actress for her performance in *L.A. Confidential* (1997).

Some family members recommended Basinger buy the small town of Braselton, Georgia in 1989 for US$20 million, to establish as a tourist attraction with movie studios and film festival, but she met financial difficulties and sold it in 1993. In a 1998 interview with Barbara Walters, Basinger admitted that "nothing good came out of it" because a rift resulted within her family. She filed for bankruptcy in 1993. Her financial difficulties were exacerbated when she pulled out of the controversial film Boxing Helena, resulting in the studio's winning an US$8-million judgment against her.

*O*n close rapport and discussion with investors who have become victims rather than victors in the investment market place, we came to discover that most investors lose not because they do not know how to invest but because they do not appreciate how not to go about investing.

In the words of Samuel Smiles, "... *we often discover what will do by finding out what will not do...*" Listed below are five ways not to go about investing.

Don't invest without a purpose: It has been said that when the purpose (of a thing) is not defined, abuse is inevitable. The same applies to investing. Many have lost and will lose while trying to invest because they do not have or do not create for themselves a purpose for investing.

It is as simple as you leaving home without a destination in mind; you would obviously end up nowhere.

Ask yourself purpose questions like: Why am I investing? How much do I intend to make? How soon do I want my returns? What do I intend to achieve by taking this investment decision?

Don't invest without knowledge and information: Knowledge (of the investment option) remains the singular most important factor required for profitable investing. Knowledge defined, is the technical knowhow of the investment option. You cannot prove to have knowledge of an investment if you do not have a good, sound understanding of the fundamentals of that investment at the very least. The fundamentals are the foundational knowledge upon which others are built. It remains of priority importance and very necessary.

Because the value of your investment will always fluctuate based on information available, it is important to be adequately informed and be abreast of happenings where you have invested your money. The ability to source information has now become an invaluable skill to an active investor.

Don't invest without proper analysis: A single piece of information could have an implication on ten different sectors. To some, it may be good and others bad; the implication is coded within the information. Because of this, most information has to be debugged and decoded before it can be used.

This process of debugging is what is known as analysis. An investor must unpardonably be skilled in information analysis because a lack of analytical ingenuity has led to the huge capital losses suffered by investors. Furthermore, don't base your investment decision on improperly analyzed information because it is one thing to analyze and another to analyze properly.

Don't invest based on popular opinion: One of the most incredible things that investors do and that is seemingly becoming an 'investment strategy' is to follow popular opinion i.e. what other people are putting money in. This is absolutely ridiculous; the 'band wagon mentality', as it is known in other quarters, is the cause of most contemporary losses experienced in various investment options.

Nobody wants to do the thinking for himself anymore; everybody wants to know what is in vogue, where the mass is heading without considering that the promoters of the theory of abnormality have proposed that the mass is, most often than not, always heading in the wrong direction. Investing based on popular opinion is suicidal and gain will only be co-incidental if they come.

To forestall the temptation of using this absurd investment strategy, you should radically increase your knowledge and improve on your analysis skills.

Don't invest based on emotion: Because I like automobiles so I should invest in an automobile business; since I love eating a lot, I would make a good restaurateur. Oh! I just love everything about that bank; I think I'd just invest in their shares.

Investing by emotion is such common philosophy and a common route to making bad investments. Your emotional attachment to anything should not in any way interfere with your investment decisions. Always keep you emotion under control; do not let it control you. If you happen to invest in any venture you are emotionally inclined too, let it be just an inevitable coincidence that resulted from careful analysis and sound counsel.

FURTHER READING

*H*aving read this book this far, it is our belief that you would have learnt key personal finance lessons that would have improved your money management skills by several points. Cases have been made for and the importance of significant concepts like insurance, investing and financial planning have been enumerated.

This book however does not go into deep detail on any of these financial planning imperatives, understandably because they are not the specific subject matter of this book. However, the following books also published by Stakes Capital Ltd and authored by Kehinde and Taiwo Sanyaolu address some of these concepts in more detail.

It is advised that you read this book [Hole in the pocket Millionaires] with the listed books to have a more rounded grasp of managing your personal finance and securing a desirable financial future.

INVESTING ACCORDING TO STAKES

'Investing According to Stakes' is a book on definitive investing. It presents a comprehensive thought on investing using an anatomical analysis of four investing pillars. The book is simple yet radically impressive of the need to make basic investment knowledge intelligible among investors.

'Investing According to Stakes' is borne out of a desire to

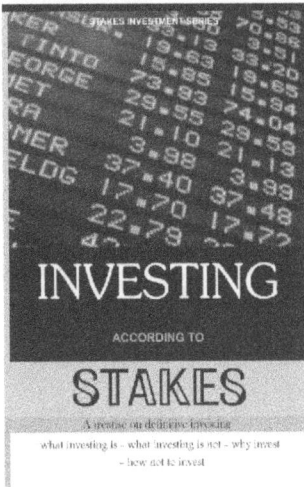

clarify the investment concept right from its definition. The book is simple yet radically impressive of the need to make basic investment knowledge intelligible among investors.

It unbundles investing into four (4) critically important definitive concepts and these form the four chapters into which the book is divided. These four pillars are: W hat Investing Is, What Investing is not, Why Invest and How not to Invest.

INSURING WEALTH

Insuring Wealth is a compendious yet broadly educating intelligible piece that expounds on an age old concept of guarding financial resources from the ever present risk of loss to accidents and unpredictable cataclysms.

In here, we explore how the financial burden of replacing property lost to accidents can easily be shifted to a third party by adopting this simple financial concept in advance. We carefully ensure that without fail you appreciate how insurance, often disregarded and mostly ignorantly

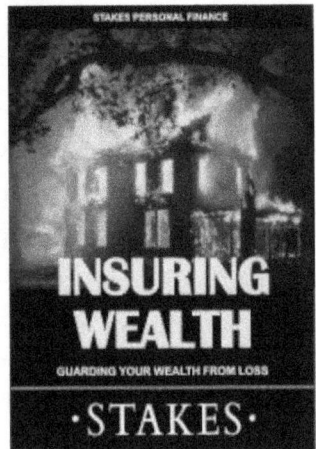

shrugged, can help you achieve a reposeful financial life.

The book which is the first in the Stakes Personal finance series, takes the model of an 'insurance for dummies', presented in an extremely lucid manner for easy comprehension.

BECOME A MARKET WIZARD

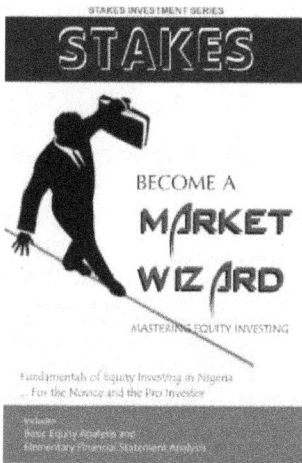

Become a Market Wizard is about the first book wholly dedicated to promoting fundamental knowledge of the working of the equity investment market in Nigeria. The book finds strength and primary purpose in the need to forestall the continuous loss of hard earned funds invested without knowledge in the capital market while also promoting investment knowledge.

The book offers an intelligible platform for the advancement of equity investment knowledge among Nigerians through its well articulated content.

The book is divided into 7 parts, each addressing specific segments of equity investing arranged in an order that allows for effective knowledge building and coherent assimilation.

The book covers topics including; purpose and essence of investing, rudiments of investing, company structure, fundamentals of equity investing, the Nigerian Stock Exchange, basic equity analysis and elementary financial statement analysis.

the authors

Sanyaolu Kehinde and Taiwo aka Stakes are the Founders of Stakes Capital Ltd and its research subsidiary International Corporate Research, the Stakes are business and investment aficionados with an enviable research knack. They are self trained experts in the rudiments of investing and the fundamentals of equity investing.

Research analysts of repute, the 'Stakes' have a natural talent for research and training and have provided solutions to clients of all classes in model design, developing evaluation frameworks, corporate assessment, industry benchmarking and project impact assessment.

They are the authors of Insuring Wealth - a book on fundamental insurance; Become a market wizard – a book on the fundamentals of equity investing and Investing according to Stakes – a definitive investing treatise. They have also authored numerous published articles and research reports which cut across diverse sectors and countries on the African continent and are driven by a purpose to ensure the promotion of knowledge in all fields of endeavor. They have a firm belief that a revolution can only come to a nation if and only if there is a people revolution (a change in the mental state of its people).

The 'Stakes' are also very compassionate businessmen who believe in a unique brand of social capitalism that wealth should be used to pursue just causes. They have an obsession for clean environments and received the maiden award of the Centre for Values in Leadership club member of the month for their contributions towards cleaning up of dirty communities in Lagos, Nigeria.

sources

cnbc.com

wikipedia.com

investopedia.com

Business Insider

Micheal Jackson: Alive or Dead

China Economic Quarterl

For further information on how to purchase our other books
or need a one on one advisory service please use the
following contacts:

website: www.hipmillionaires.com
www.stakescapital.com

Email: coach@hipmillionaires.com
letstalk@stakescapital.com

Phone: +2348060043692
+2348054061133

www.ingramcontent.com/pod-product-compliance
Lightning Source LLC
Chambersburg PA
CBHW022047190326
41520CB00008B/730